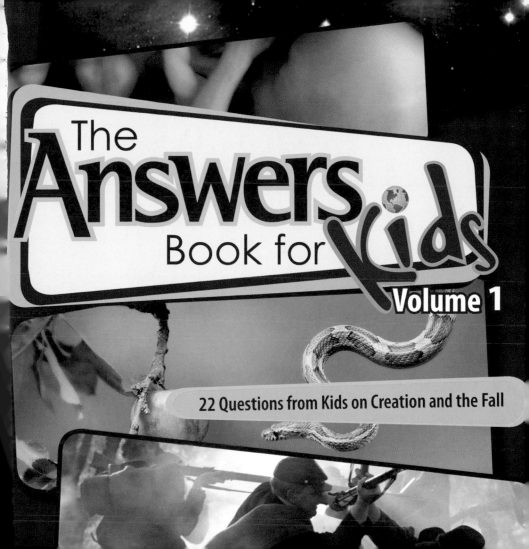

The
Answers
Book for Kids
Volume 1

22 Questions from Kids on Creation and the Fall

Master Books®
P.O. Box 726
Green Forest, AR 72638

Master Books® is a division of the New Leaf Publishing Group, Inc.

Printed in China

Cover Design by Rebekah Krall
Interior Design by Terry White

ISBN 13: 978-0-89051-526-6
Library of Congress number: 2008904921

All Scripture references are New King James Version unless otherwise noted.

Please visit our website for other great titles: www.masterbooks.net

When you see this icon, there will be related Scripture references noted for parents to use in answering their children's, and even their own, questions.

For Parents and Teachers

Dear Moms and Dads:

The more I learn about our infinite Creator God, and the longer I serve Him, the more amazed I am at His greatness. As I consider the universe God created, I share David's exclamation in Psalm 145:3, *"Great is the LORD, and greatly to be praised; And His greatness is unsearchable."*

The greatness of God is truly unsearchable when we consider creation. This book is intended to give biblical and scientific answers, in a way children will understand, to questions they have about God's creation and man's fall into sin.

Sadly, our culture today, by and large, has turned away from the truth of God's Word in Genesis. As you know, the Bible makes it very clear that parents are responsible for the teaching of their children. I thank you for allowing me the opportunity to partner with you as we strive to teach children to not only believe God's Word, but to also put their faith and trust in our Savior — the Creator of the universe — Jesus Christ.

Charles Spurgeon once said, "The only way to keep chaff out of the child's cup is to fill it brimful with good wheat." We need to be consistent and intentional as we fill the "cups" of children with the "good wheat" of God's precious, holy Word.

My prayer is that this book will begin to answer many of the questions your children will encounter, but in a way that gives God the glory, honor, and power He is worthy of.

Ken Ham
President/CEO, Answers in Genesis

3

Question: When did time begin?

Sarah S.

Age 10 — Canada

In the beginnin

4

Answer:

In the beginning God created the heavens and the earth (Genesis 1:1).

Time began when God started to create everything in the whole universe. He did this "in the beginning" of the Creation Week. According to the Bible, that was about 6,000 years ago. Before then, there were no days or weeks or years. It is hard for us to understand, but time, just like everything else God created, including you and me, had a beginning, and it wasn't very long ago! God, on the other hand, is infinite. He has always existed, and He is not bound to time, like we are. In fact, the Bible says that to God a day can be like 1,000 years and 1,000 years can be just like a day. Time just doesn't mean the same thing to God as it does to us. He's "outside" of it. We do know, however that He created time on the first day of creation.

2 Peter 3:8; Revelation 1:8

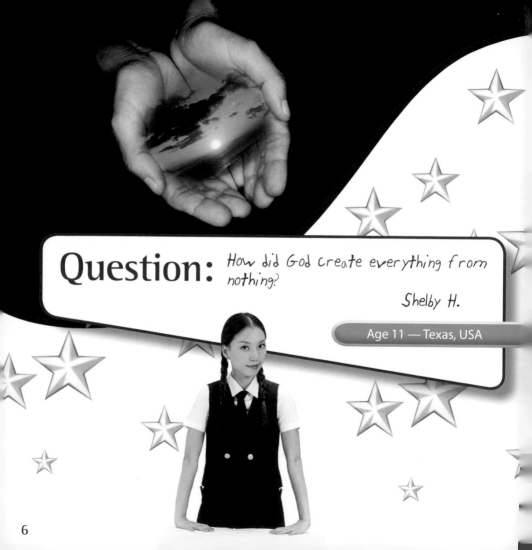

Question: How did God create everything from nothing?

Shelby H.

Age 11 — Texas, USA

6

Answer:

By faith we understand that the worlds were framed by the word of God, so that the things which are seen were not made of things which are visible (Hebrews 11:3).

We serve a mighty and powerful God! He created everything — the whole universe — in just six days! And in our Bible verse we learn that the things we see were made from things not seen, or invisible things. In other words, there was nothing (or maybe we should say "not even nothing") when God began to create.

If you read the first chapter of Genesis, you will see the words "God said" eight times. Shelby, this explains how God created by His great power. For example, can you imagine how amazing it must have been when God said, "Let there be lights in the heavens?" The stars, sun, and moon appeared, just as God had planned. God needed only to speak and everything was created. He truly is worthy of our praise!

Exodus 20:11; Genesis 1:14–15

Question: Did Adam and Eve have bellybuttons?

Kimberly W.

8

Answer:

And the LORD God formed man of the dust of the ground . . . and man became a living being. . . . Then the rib which the LORD God had taken from man He made into a woman (Genesis 2:7, 22).

You are not the first one to wonder about Adam's bellybutton! Do you know that our bellybuttons are scars left over from when we were born? When a baby is growing in her mommy's tummy, she needs food. She gets food through a cord attached to her mommy. We all needed that cord in order to survive and grow! Our bellybuttons are scars from the cord that once fed us.

The Bible tells us that our great God made the first man (Adam) directly out of dust. He was already an adult, so he didn't need a cord to get food. The Bible also tells us that God made the first woman (Eve) directly from the rib of the man. So she was an adult too. I think it is very possible they did not have or need bellybuttons.

Genesis 2:4–7, 15–23

Question: Where is the Garden of Eden?

Joy B.

Age 10 — Michigan, USA

10

Answer:

A river watering the garden flowed from Eden; from there it was separated into four headwaters. The name of the first is Pishon. . . . The name of the second river is the Gihon. . . . The name of the third river is the Tigris. . . . And the fourth river is the Euphrates (Genesis 2:10–14 NIV).

Joy, we have absolutely no idea where the Garden of Eden was located. The Bible verse tells us about the Garden of Eden and it even mentions four rivers around the Garden. But there are only two rivers today that have the same names as those where the Garden of Eden was located, the Tigris and the Euphrates; the rest of the description doesn't match. So the Garden of Eden wasn't there.

Also, the worldwide flood of Noah's day would have destroyed everything on the earth, including the Garden of Eden. So why do those two rivers have the same names? Well, I think Noah, or someone in his family, named the rivers. And he used names of rivers that existed before the Flood — names he already knew. Maybe he wanted to be sure that the people would not forget the days before the Flood, and to remind them they must honor and obey God.

Genesis 7:18–23

Question:

Does Genesis 1:1-2 refer to the first day?

Lee R.

Age 9 — New York, USA

Answer:

So the evening and the morning were the first day (Genesis 1:5).

Yes, Lee, the first two verses of Genesis 1 describe events on the very same day. I presume you ask the question because you have heard that supposedly millions of years passed between verses 1 and 2. You can find the answer to this question if you read closely what Genesis, God's Holy Word, says.

When God first began to create, He created the heavens and the earth. That's verse 1. They weren't completed yet. Verse 2 describes what they looked like so far. The earth was "without form and void" (without life and incomplete). Each day God completed a bit more until, after six days, it was all finished. He called His finished work "very good."

And Lee, you need to know there are many qualified creation scientists who do not believe in millions of years and who have done much scientific research that confirms the universe is only thousands of years old. When you read the Bible carefully, there is no doubt that verses 1 and 2 describe part of the first day.

Genesis 1:1–5

13

Question:

When God created the earth, were the trees fully grown, or were they baby trees? If they were full grown, did they have growth rings?

Chris J.

Age 11— California, USA

14

Answer:

And the earth brought forth grass, the herb that yields seed according to its kind, and the tree that yields fruit, whose seed is in itself according to its kind. And God saw that it was good (Genesis 1:12).

Well, let's see. We know by our Bible verse that the trees in the Garden provided fruit for food. And we know that Adam and Eve could eat the fruit from all the trees except one. They didn't need to wait for years for the trees to grow big enough to produce fruit, did they?

It seems that God created the trees to sprout, grow, and bear fruit all in one day. I do believe that the trees had growth rings, for a couple of reasons. First, they were fully grown trees to start with, and most grown trees have growth rings. Second, the growth rings of many trees are actually part of the structure of the tree and support the tree. Some trees would need those growth rings to stand tall and produce fruit for Adam and Eve. So the growth rings were part of what made these trees perfect and very good, like the rest of God's creation.

Genesis 1:29–31

Question: Why did God make a week seven days long?

Caleb F.

Age 6 — Ohio, USA

16

Answer:

For in six days the LORD made the heavens and the earth, the sea, and all that is in them, and rested the seventh day. Therefore the LORD blessed the Sabbath day and hallowed it (Exodus 20:11).

Our Bible verse tells us why God made the week seven days long. Let me explain. He made the seven-day week just for us. He created everything in six days and rested on the seventh day, right? Well, God could have made the entire universe in one split second because He is all-powerful and mighty. But He was setting a pattern for us to follow.

If we just kept on working every single day, we would get very tired and probably get sick. God was showing us that we can work six days, but then we need to rest for one day. Remember that He didn't need to take that long to create everything (and He didn't need to rest). Six days is actually a very long time for God. The seven-day week is for us!

Exodus 16:25–27

17

Question: Why was the first person that God created a boy?

Chloe G.

Age 6 — Illinois, USA

18

Answer:

And the LORD God said, "It is not good that man should be alone; I will make him a helper comparable to him" (Genesis 2:18).

Okay. First of all, this person wasn't exactly a boy. Adam was a man. And we know that, as our infinite Creator, God can do whatever He wants to do. When He made Adam first, God was teaching us how He wanted our families to be. He made Adam to be the head of the family. See in our Bible verse? It says that God wanted to create a "helper" for Adam, so He created Eve. Eve was the perfect complement to Adam.

Adam was the leader of that very first family. Adam was not better or more valuable than Eve. It was just that God knew someone had to be the leader, so He made that leader Adam. By doing this, God showed us that He wants the husband, the dad in the family, to be the spiritual leader in the family.

Ephesians 5:22–25; 1 Corinthians 11:3

Question: Why did God let Adam name the animals? Why didn't He name them himself?

Caleb Z.

Age 11 — Tennessee, USA

Answer:

And the Lord God said, "It is not good that man should be alone; I will make him a helper comparable to him" (Genesis 2:18).

Our Bible verse says that God didn't think it was good for man to be alone. If you keep reading in your Bible, you'll see that the Lord brought animals He had already created to Adam. Now we know that God easily could have named all of those animals. But God was teaching Adam and us a lesson.

You see, as Adam was naming the animals, it became very clear to him that he was completely different from the animals and was a special creation. He was created in God's very image. Keep this in mind, Caleb, when you hear that humans evolved from animals. God's Word tells us just the opposite! Humans are far different from animals, and when Adam understood that he was alone, God put him to sleep to make a "helper" for him, and her name was Eve!

Genesis 2:19–25

Question: Did Adam give each of the animals the names we call them today?

Olivia B.

Age 7 — Pennsylvania, USA

22

Answer:

So Adam gave names to all cattle, to the birds of the air, and to every beast of the field (Genesis 2:20).

This question has a couple of answers. Let me explain.

First, Adam didn't name every animal created or each variety and species. He would have only named the "kinds" of animals that God brought to him. (All of the varieties and species would not have been there yet!) In other words, he only named the dog kind, the cat kind, the horse kind, etc.

Second, we don't know what language Adam spoke, so there is really no way of knowing what he called each animal kind. And third, when God later confused all the languages at the Tower of Babel, it is possible that Adam's original language did not survive (if it had survived, we still wouldn't know what it was). As we study the Bible, we see that there is no way of knowing what Adam called the animals. But the names were probably not the same as today. Like for example, the word "dinosaurs." The word wasn't even invented until 1841, but we know from the Bible that these creatures were created along with the other animal kinds. But we do not know the name Adam gave them.

Genesis 11:7–9

23

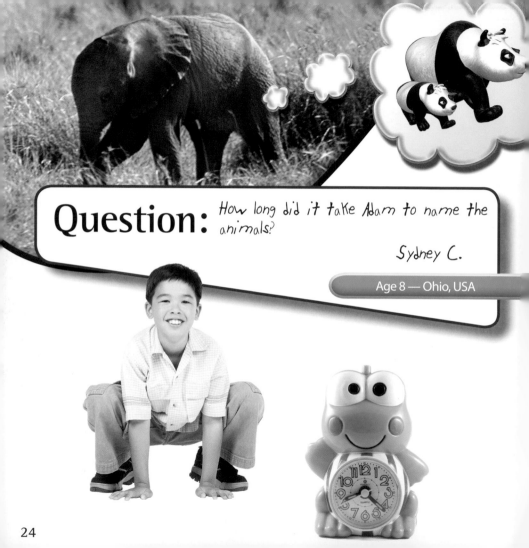

Question: How long did it take Adam to name the animals?

Sydney C.

Age 8 — Ohio, USA

24

Answer:

...and [God] brought them to Adam to see what he would call them . . . (Genesis 2:19).

Well, a lot of people say there is no way Adam could have had enough time to name all the animals in a single day. Actually, when we read God's Word carefully, we find he didn't name all the animals.

First, we know from Genesis that Adam named only land animals on the sixth day (and he named them before Eve was created on that same day, by the way). This means that he definitely named them within 24 hours, at most!

Second, remember from the previous question that Adam named only "kinds" of land animals and then, only the cattle, birds of the air, and beast of the fields. Adam really named far fewer animals than we think! One more thing — Adam was the most intelligent man that ever lived. God made him with a perfect brain and a perfect memory. It wouldn't take him long to think of the names and to then remember which animal was which! He had plenty of intelligence and plenty of time to name them all in one day!

Genesis 2:18–20

Question: The serpent talked to Eve, so why can't snakes talk today?

Jemimah F.

Age 10 — Northern Ireland

Answer:

So the donkey said to Balaam, "Am I not your donkey on which you have ridden, ever since I became yours, to this day? Was I ever disposed to do this to you?" (Numbers 22:30).

You, Jemimah, are made in God's image, right? You can talk and communicate. You can have a conversation with other human beings (also created in God's image). Animals are not made in the image of God. And yet, you see in our Bible verse that God opened the mouth of a donkey and it talked.

Whenever it will serve God's perfect plan, He can use anything to convey His message, even a donkey.

In the same way, God allowed Satan (the devil) to use the serpent to disguise himself and tempt Eve.

Genesis 3:1–7

27

Question:

Why did God put the tree in the Garden of Eden if He didn't want Adam and Eve to eat the fruit from it?

Lance B.

Age 5 — Kansas, USA

28

Answer:

. . . but of the tree of the knowledge of good and evil you shall not eat, for in the day that you eat of it you shall surely die (Genesis 2:17).

Have you ever played with a puppet? The puppet will do whatever you want it to do because it is on your hand. You are moving it, talking for it, and making it sit, stand, and dance. Well, when God made Adam, He didn't want him to be a puppet, but He wanted Adam to truly love Him.

The command about the tree of the knowledge of good and evil was God's test to see if Adam really did love God enough to totally obey Him. But Adam failed the test. He sinned against God and did something God told him not to do. This was a very bad day for all of us because Adam was the head of the whole human race — the very first man. When he failed God's test, he brought sin into the world, and now all of us have the same sin nature from Adam.

John 3:16; Romans 5:12

Question: If all that God created was good, how could Satan be bad?

Jordan C.

Age 7 — Indiana, USA

Answer:

Then God saw everything that He had made, and indeed it was very good. So the evening and the morning were the sixth day (Genesis 1:31).

The Bible clearly tells us that on Day 6, when God saw all He had made, He called it all "very good." God had to have included the angels with the rest of creation! So Lucifer (or Satan) was very good when God created him. In fact, Lucifer was one of the beautiful angels God had created!

But he soon became proud and wanted to take God's place on His throne. He thought that he could be as great as God. Because God created Adam and Eve as special human beings, Satan wanted them to turn away from God, too. So he told Eve that she could become like God. They believed him, sinned, and were cast out of the Garden.

Isaiah 14:13; James 1:13–15

Question: Who was Cain's wife? Why doesn't the Bible mention her birth if she was Eve's baby?

Calista M.

Age 8 — New Hampshire, US

32

Answer:

After he begot Seth, the days of Adam were eight hundred years; and he had sons and daughters (Genesis 5:4).

Adam and Eve had many children. Adam lived to be 930 years old, and Jewish tradition states that he had 33 sons and 23 daughters. (That is a really big family!)

Most people believe that Cain married his sister or his niece, and the Bible does not tell us what her name was. Keep in mind that way back then (about 6,000 years ago) close relatives could marry — they had to in order to start their own families. Even Abraham married his half-sister. Of course, we can't do that anymore because of the effects of sin on our bodies and because God told Moses that people were not to marry close relatives from that time on. Now when we marry, we marry someone not so closely related to us.

While we're speaking about marriage, Calista, remember that according to God, marriage is one man and one woman until death — that's how God commands it.

Genesis 2:24, 20:12; Leviticus 18:6

Question:

Did bumblebees have stingers before Adam and Eve sinned?

Heidi C.

Age 10 — Ohio, USA

34

Answer:

For we know that the whole creation groans and labors with birth pangs together until now (Romans 8:22).

Because of Adam's sin in the Garden, we do not live in a perfect world. We really can't imagine what a perfect world would be like. We know there was no violence and no death — we wouldn't expect this from a loving, life-giving God.

Our Scripture verse tells us that the whole creation is affected by sin, and that includes bumblebees. So, when we consider their stingers, all of us wonder the same thing that you've asked, Heidi. I think it is likely that the bumblebees had what we now call stingers before sin, but they weren't used to harm anything. I am sure they weren't originally meant to sting us, but because of sin in the world, things have changed! When a bumblebee reacts to us in a fallen world, it hurts!

Genesis 3:8–19

Question: How long were Adam and Eve in the Garden of Eden before they sinned?

Olivia K.

Age 11 — Australia

36

Answer:

Then God blessed them, and God said to them, "Be fruitful and multiply . . ." (Genesis 1:28).

Olivia, let's look at what the Bible says to find an answer. Our verse says that God told Adam and Eve to be fruitful and multiply. In other words, they were supposed to start a family in the Garden. But the Bible also indicates that they had to leave before they had any children.

You see, the Bible tells us that all men are born with the sin of Adam. If Adam and Eve had started their family in the Garden, their children would not have been born in sin or affected by Adam's sin. So, I think they may have been in the Garden only a few days before they sinned and God made them leave.

Romans 3:23, 5:12

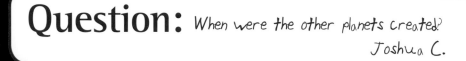

Question: When were the other planets created?

Joshua C.

Age 8 — Arkansas, USA

Answer:

Then God made two great lights: the greater light to rule the day, and the lesser light to rule the night. He made the stars also. . . . So the evening and the morning were the fourth day (Genesis 1:16, 19).

Our Bible verse tells us that God made the sun, moon, and stars on the fourth day. Although the Bible doesn't specifically say "planets," it is correct to say that the Hebrew word translated "star" included the planets that God spoke into existence on that great day!

God also tells us that He hung these "lights" in the heavens for signs, seasons, days, and years. And another fun fact we find, as we read Genesis 1, is that the earth is actually three days older than all the stars and planets, since the earth was created on Day 1!

Psalm 19:1, 33:6

39

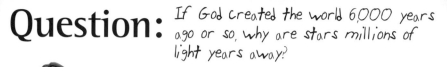

Question:

If God created the world 6,000 years ago or so, why are stars millions of light years away?

Brendon M.

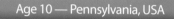

Age 10 — Pennsylvania, USA

Answer:

The heavens declare the glory of God; and the firmament shows His handiwork (Psalm 19:1).

Brendon, what a question! Yes, we know from the dates God gives us in the Bible that He did create the whole universe about 6,000 years ago. When we hear the term light-year, we need to realize it is not a measure of time but a measure of distance, telling us how far away something is. Distant stars and galaxies might be millions of light-years away, but that doesn't mean that it took millions of years for the light to get here, it just means it is really far away!

When God created the universe, everything was already working perfectly, exactly how He wanted it to work. So, I believe the stars could be seen (however God did that) on earth as soon as God spoke them into existence. Keep enjoying the splendor of the night sky, but remember that God created it to display His glory so we could behold how wonderful and powerful our Creator really is!

Psalm 50:6, 147:4; Isaiah 40:26

Question: What is evolution?

Calista J.

Age 8 — New Hampshire, USA

42

Answer:

So God created great sea creatures and every living thing that moves, with which the waters abounded, according to their kind, and every winged bird according to its kind. And God saw that it was good (Genesis 1:21).

Calista, the word evolution actually just means "change." Of course, we all know in our world today it usually means something else. When most people hear the word evolution today, they think of Charles Darwin. Darwin believed that one kind of animal evolved into a totally different kind and that eventually ape-like creatures evolved into human beings over millions of years.

This is totally against God's Word, which clearly records that God created all living things according to their kinds (that dogs would only produce dogs, cats only produce cats, and so on). God's Word also states that the first man was made from dust and the first woman from his side (they didn't come from ape-like creatures)! There has never been any scientific evidence to show that one kind of animal (any animal) has ever turned into another totally different kind of animal! God's Word is true.

Romans 1:22; Psalm 8:3–9; Genesis 1:20–25

Question:

Why do evolutionists trust their beliefs and not Christ?

Joy B.

Age 11 — Michigan, USA

Faith

Answer:

But they deliberately forget that long ago by God's word the heavens existed and the earth was formed out of water and by water (2 Peter 3:5 NIV).

God's Word gives us the answer to your question, Joy. Our Scripture verse says that people "deliberately forget" that God created the universe from nothing, that He spoke it all into existence.

Why don't they believe? Why do they want to forget? We are all born sinners and because of that people just don't want to admit that a powerful, all-knowing God created them. They don't want to admit that God is in control of all things — even them!

They would rather believe that they evolved from slime over millions of years. If this were true, then it means they don't owe God anything. They don't have to obey Him or be grateful for His many gifts. But the Bible makes it very clear that God is our Creator; we are His, and He has a plan for our life. He is the One we need to listen to and obey!

Job 42:2; Ephesians 1:11; Genesis 1:20–25

Question: Did God use the same design for humans as for monkeys?

Caleb W.

46

Answer:

Then God said, "Let Us make man in Our image, according to Our likeness" (Genesis 1:26).

Have you ever gone shopping and seen a whole bunch of really neat skateboards? You might know what type they are because of how they are painted or designed. They are similar because the same company made them. Well, when you look at God's creation, you find many similarities because the same Maker created them.

God created all living things, and it makes sense that a lot of these share many similar characteristics or design. The same God, the same Designer, created both monkeys and humans and thus there are some similarities. But the differences are also important. Man is not an animal! Our Bible verse here says that man was made in God's image — a monkey wasn't.

Man is very different from a monkey. Man can think, he can appreciate and write music, and he can build airplanes and bridges. Monkeys can't do this. Humans can have a relationship with their God, and we can spend eternity with Him if we believe His Word concerning salvation. We can ask forgiveness for our sins and believe in Jesus Christ, who took the punishment for our sins. Monkeys and animals cannot do that!

Psalm 104; 1 John 3:1; John 1:12

HOLY BIBLE